ICE CLIMBING

ADVENTURE SPORTS

ICE
CLIMBING

SCOTT WURDINGER & LESLIE RAPPARLIE

CREATIVE EDUCATION

Published by Creative Education
123 South Broad Street, Mankato, Minnesota 56001
Creative Education is an imprint of the The Creative
Company

Design and production by Blue Design
(www.bluedes.com)
Art direction by Rita Marshall

Photographs by Alamy (Alaska Stock LLC, blickwinkel, John
Digby, DPB images, Vick Fisher, Gavin Gough, nick hore,
Brian Horisk, Peter Jennings, maurice joseph, Nic Cleave
Photography, Photo Network, Pep Roig, Simon Vine,
StockShot, Ron Yue), Vertical Perceptions

Printed in the United States of America

Library of Congress Cataloging-in-Publication Data

Wurdinger, Scott D.
Ice climbing / by Scott Wurdinger and Leslie Rapparlie.
p. cm. — (Adventure sports)
Includes bibliographical references and index.
ISBN-13 : 978-1-58341-393-7
1. Snow and ice climbing—Juvenile literature. I. Title. II.
Series. (Mankato, Minn.)

GV200.3.W87 2005
796.52'23—dc22   2005050685

First edition

9 8 7 6 5 4 3 2 1

ICE CLIMBING

The air is cold, with a slight breeze from the northwest, as two climbers push upward along a winding mountain trail. Fresh snow crunches beneath their heavy boots as the terrain levels out. The climbers look at each other with growing excitement. Before them stands a giant tower of blue ice, formed by a waterfall that appears to have frozen in midair.

The climbers stop—they have come to conquer this frozen mass. Shrugging off their heavy packs, they strap crampons to the bottom of their boots and grab sharp ice tools with their gloved hands. They tie a colorful climbing rope to their harnesses. After double-checking that everything is in order, one of them gracefully swings her ice tool, aiming for the heart of the ice. With a perfect thud, the tool locks into place. The climber lifts one foot onto the ice; the points on the front of the boot stick into the frozen water.

In the beginning, climbing ice aided mountaineers and scientists in the exploration of Arctic regions, glaciers in Alaska and South America, and various mountain ranges. Today, ice climbing is one of the fastest-growing adventure sports.

Ice climbers thrive in frigid temperatures that transform waterfalls into vertical ice formations. Overhanging ice and ice caves, such as those on the Brunt Ice Shelf in Antarctica, are the types of challenges climbers aspire to tackle.

Slowly, she moves upward, swinging her ice tools and moving her feet. Her heart pounds, and her breath comes in fast puffs, partly from exertion and partly from nerves. Finally, she slides over the top of the frozen waterfall and peers out over a serene world of ice and snow. The climber raises her arms in victory. Although she has summited waterfalls before, a successful climb still thrills her.

Every year, ice climbers around the world await the arrival of winter, and with it, the opportunity to scale frozen waterfalls. These adrenaline-loving adventurers thrive on the extreme nature of their sport—its frigid temperatures, slippery walls, and physical challenges. Many ice climbers also relish the peace they find against quiet ice on a mountainside. As nature lover John Muir wrote of the peace of the mountains: "[It] will flow into you as the sunshine flows into trees. The winds will blow their own freshness into you, and the storms their energy, while cares will drop off like autumn leaves."

Climbing ice is usually a winter activity. However, in Alaska, where there are mild summer temperatures—even in June and July—and summer sunlight almost 24 hours a day, climbing glaciers and ice formations is a year-round sport.

A History on Ice

Fewer than 100 years ago, climbing ice meant ascending low- to moderate-angled ice fields and glaciers high up on the side of a mountain. Ice climbing then had a strictly practical application: to ascend steep ice in order to reach the summit of a mountain. Today, the term "ice climbing" has an entirely different meaning. Many serious ice climbers have no interest in carrying a heavy pack on a multi-day expedition to reach the peak of a mountain. Instead, most climbers today seek the challenge and thrill of climbing vertical frozen waterfalls or similar man-made ice routes. The evolution from climbing glaciers to scaling waterfalls occurred relatively quickly, sped along by advances in equipment, as well as by adventurous climbers who pushed the limits of the sport.

Ice climbing dates back to 1908, when British mountaineer Oscar Eckenstein developed the first crampons that connected to the bottom of mountaineering boots. Eckenstein's unique crampons had sharp, teeth-like spikes that pierced the ice and allowed climbers to simply walk up slippery slopes, eliminating the arduous task of cutting steps into hard ice and snow. Later, in 1932, German inventor Laurent Grivel designed a crampon with an additional two front teeth protruding from the toe of the boot, which allowed climbers to face the ice and thrust their toes forward into it.

This invention transformed ice climbing by enabling climbers to front point up vertical ice for the first time.

In the late 1960s, famous American ice climber Yvon Chouinard started experimenting with equipment designs, shortening the handle of ice axes and redesigning the curve of their picks to make the axes easier to grip and more effective at biting into the ice. Chouinard's designs led climbing equipment companies to develop new, lightweight ice tools, ice axes, and ice screws, making it possible to climb higher and harder routes.

In 1974, two American climbers, Jeff Lowe and Mike Weiss, revolutionized the sport when they summited Bridal Veil Falls—one of the most difficult frozen waterfalls in the United States—near Telluride, Colorado. Lowe and Weiss made history by becoming the first climbers to reach the top of the 5,000-foot (1,525 m) waterfall. Their climb created a new mindset among ice climbers, who saw for the first time that it was possible to scale the vertical and overhanging ice of frozen waterfalls.

Rare formations in the ice, as well as sheer steepness, made Bridal Veil Falls in Colorado the most difficult ice climb in the U.S. for almost 10 years. Because of this formation's risky nature, the city of Telluride, Colorado, regulates the number of climbers that are able to ascend every year.

The adventurous sport of ice climbing continued to grow, and in the early 1990s, visionaries such as Eric Jacobsen, Gary Wild, and Bill Whitt—all from Ouray, Colorado—donated time and money to create a series of man-made frozen waterfalls in the Uncompahgre Gorge in the Rocky Mountains of Colorado. The men set up a system of hoses, valves, showerheads, and timers to spray water from a pipeline on top of the gorge down the sides of its cliffs, where it froze, creating a number of new climbs. This area soon became the first man-made ice park in the U.S. Today, Ouray Ice Park has some of the best ice climbing in the world and attracts around 15,000 climbers a year.

While ice parks offer controlled ice climbs, many adventure climbers travel to exotic locations to experience natural ice wonders. The Andes mountain range in Ecuador offers climbers the opportunity to scale a volcano's frozen slopes.

Tools of The Trade

Moser Quark, Fusion Leashless, Diamond Viper, Warthog, Snarg—they sound more like video games than the names of modern technical ice tools and screws, but radical changes in equipment designs deserve radical names. In the not-too-distant past, ice climbers used long, wood-handled ice axes and heavy steel crampons to climb steep ice fields. Today, technology and advances in equipment and clothing have reshaped the sport, enabling climbers to safely scale higher and more intense routes.

It would be next to impossible for climbers to grab slippery ice with their bare hands. Instead, climbers grip ice tools, which they swing into the ice. An ice tool consists of a shaft, a pick, and an adze or hammer. The shaft, usually made of aluminum alloy coated with rubber, is lightweight and strong, while the curved, toothed pick bites securely into the ice. Most tools used for scaling vertical ice are around 20 inches (50 cm) long, with a curved shaft. Many ice tools today come with an array of specialized features, such as ergonomic grips, pinky protectors (to keep the little finger from smashing into the ice), sharper-angled heads that bite into the ice more easily with less force, and jagged teeth that give the tool maximum grab on ice. Some tools—such as the Moser Quark and Diamond Viper—can be equipped with a leash, which attaches the tool to the climber's wrist, but tools without

leashes—such as the Fusion Leashless—are becoming more popular, as they allow climbers more freedom of movement. With such variety in design and features, ice tools generally range from $200 to $400 apiece.

Crampons are also necessary for ice climbing, as they help climbers jab their feet securely into the ice. The first crampons were designed for walking on flat snow and ice and had 10 points that faced downward under the feet. These crampons were typically built with four points under the heel and six under the front half of the foot. Such crampons had a hinge in the center that allowed the foot to bend and flex. They attached to mountaineering boots with long straps and were tightly buckled on the side of the foot.

Modern crampons have an additional two points that stick out in the front and are angled downward so that the climber can kick forward into the ice and stand up with his or her weight on these two points. Today's crampons are usually rigid as opposed to hinged, which places less stress on the calf and lower leg muscles, allowing climbers to be more efficient and conserve leg strength when climbing vertical ice. In recent years, the evolution of ice climbing competitions has pushed crampon development even further. Today, climbers can purchase single-point crampons, which have only one point in the front and provide more balance and stability than other crampons. An experienced climber can also choose single-point crampons with an additional point on the back for hooking the ice with the backside of the heel.

Climbing ropes, used to secure the climber to an anchor, come in a variety of styles and lengths. The most common ice climbing rope is the 10.5-millimeter (0.4 in.), which often comes in 200-foot (60 m) pieces. "Dry" ropes are used for ice climbing because they have a protective sheath that repels water and keeps the rope relatively dry. This is important because when ropes get wet, they become heavy, making it more strenuous for the climber to lift them. Climbing ropes are incredibly strong and are rated according to the number of falls they can withstand. For example, a three-leader fall rope

Early alpinists—climbers who travel over mountains—greatly disliked the crampon when it was invented and thought of it as an "artificial aid." Wanting to keep alpine climbing "pure," they tediously cut steps when they encountered ice. Today, some of these ice steps still remain.

can withstand three significant falls by a climber without breaking. However, after the third fall, the rope should be retired since another fall on it could have deadly consequences.

For longer climbs, ice screws are necessary. These lightweight, hollow tubes made of aluminum alloy range in length from four to eight and a half inches (10–22 cm). Their razor-sharp threads bite securely into the ice. Some screws, such as the Warthog and Snarg, are pounded into the ice, while others are screwed in. Newer ice screw models have small handles that allow the climber to better grip them while twisting them into the ice.

Whenever ice screws are used, carabiners are also needed. These clips, which have a one-way, spring-loaded gate, are attached to a screw eyelet. A climbing rope is pushed through the gate, which will not open when weight is placed on the rope. For added safety, some carabiner gates can be locked shut. Made of lightweight aluminum and available in several different shapes and sizes, carabiners can typically hold 4,000 to 6,000 pounds (1,815–2,720 kg) with the gate closed.

The creation of the modern ice tool in the 1960s consisted of modifying the mountaineering ice axe by shortening the shaft and reversing the angle of the axe head. Vertical ice climbing became less difficult with the new tools.

The clothing a climber wears deserves careful consideration for the sake of safety. Wearing an absorbent material, such as cotton, can be dangerous. Cotton can become wet and heavy with sweat or melted snow and ice, and can then freeze in extreme cold.

Besides gear used on the ice, climbers must carefully choose gear for their bodies. Climbing harnesses—which consist of a waist belt and leg loops—connect a climber to the climbing rope and support him or her in the event of a fall. Helmets are another critical safety component, as their hard plastic protects the climber's head from falling ice and rock. In order to stay dry, many climbers invest in Gore-Tex for their outer layer of clothing. This lightweight fabric allows perspiration to escape through tiny pores but does not allow rain and water to penetrate. Because of its unique properties, Gore-Tex is fairly expensive—a Gore-Tex jacket can cost more than $500—but it is invaluable in keeping a climber comfortable, dry, and warm. Boots are also a must for ice climbing. Many climbers choose thick plastic boots, since they do not freeze as easily as leather boots, and opt for a Gore-Tex layer on the outside of the boot in order to keep their feet as dry as possible.

Climbing nature's ice routes is an exhilarating experience that many enjoy. In order to keep ice climbs clean and well-preserved for others, climbers practice the "leave no trace" policy. This includes being prepared, traveling durable routes, disposing of waste, and respecting all wildlife encountered.

The Way Up

Staring up at the frozen, shiny surface of a waterfall, it can be difficult to believe that such a structure can be scaled. Some sections of ice slope inward, clinging to the rock behind them, while others slope outward as though the falls froze instantly when the water catapulted off the side of the cliff.

Safely climbing such daunting ice faces requires not only an understanding of how to use all of the necessary equipment, but also a knowledge of how to perform climbing techniques. To begin a vertical climb, an ice climber swings an ice tool into the ice, listening for the thunk that signifies that the tool has been firmly planted. After securing the tool, the climber plants his or her crampons and other tool into the ice. Then, maintaining three points of contact with the ice at all times, the climber begins to move up the waterfall, constantly examining its surface to find the most stable location to place the next tool or crampon point.

As climbers work their way up the ice, they rely heavily on the strength of their legs, using their arms primarily to help maintain balance. In order to prevent "sewing machine leg," a phenomenon in which the leg begins to shake uncontrollably as a result of prolonged muscle contraction, climbers need to straighten their legs as they step up. Failing to do so could result in an unsuccessful climb, as climbers who experience sewing machine leg often have to be lowered to the ground to rest.

Successful ice climbers learn to both think in the moment and look ahead; they focus on finding good holds on the ice to establish three secure points of contact, while at the same time envisioning their next step or tool strike up the ice face.

To place ice screws, a climber scrapes away thin ice, places the screw at a downward angle, and completely tightens the screw. When it is secure, the pressure of the inserted screw should cause the ice to slightly melt.

Once a climber has learned the basics of climbing, the safest way to gain experience and practice proper climbing techniques is to climb using a top rope system. Top rope climbing involves bringing two ropes to the top of a climb (up a different route than the climb itself). One rope serves as an anchor, with each of its ends tied to a big rock or tree and its middle, tied into figure eight knots, dangling over the cliff edge. The middle of the second rope, the belay rope, is clipped with carabiners, which are then clipped to the figure eight knots in the anchor rope. Both ends of the belay rope are tossed over the edge of the cliff to the beginning of the climb far below. One end is tied to the climber, while the other is threaded through the belay device, which is clipped to the belayer. During a climb, the belayer stays at the foot of the route and takes up the slack in the rope, carefully watching the climber at all times. If the climber begins to fall, the belayer catches him or her by using the friction of the belay device to hold the rope and keep the slack from running back through the carabiner at the top of the route.

Quebec City's Montmorency Falls plunges 344 feet (105 m) over a ledge where the St. Lawrence and Montmorency Rivers converge. This spectacular waterfall offers many climbing challenges in winter. Even novices can scale the falls after attending an ice climbing course.

Once the climber reaches the top, the belayer lowers him or her to the ground by letting the rope slide back through the belay device in a controlled manner.

More experienced climbers often employ the lead climbing technique, either for a greater challenge or because there is no way to top rope the climb. This process requires a lead climber to ascend a portion of the ice face without any protection against falls. As soon as possible, the climber inserts an ice screw into the ice. Once the screw is secure, the climber connects a carabiner to it and clips the rope—which is tied to his or her harness—into the carabiner. The loose end of the rope runs down to the belayer, who takes up the slack just as in a top rope climb. On long climbs, the lead climber continues to insert screws wherever ice conditions allow. The leader needs to place screws as often as possible, since in the case of a slip, he or she will fall twice the distance from the last screw before the rope stops the fall. When the lead climber reaches the top of the route, he or she becomes the belayer as the climber at the bottom ties to the rope and climbs up the face, unscrewing the ice screws as he or she goes. To get back to the bottom, climbers generally **rappel** down the side of the ice face.

Lead climbing requires tremendous exertion, since the leader must hold on to an ice tool with one hand while screwing in an ice screw with the other. To prevent fatigue, climbers attempting **multi-pitch** climbs may reverse roles and take turns as the lead climber. One climber ascends the first **pitch**, then stops at a **belay point** and belays the other climber up. The second climber can then forge the way up the next pitch, giving the first climber a chance to rest.

The thickness and stability of ice formations can fluctuate with the weather. Many ice parks and experienced ice climbers will monitor the ice and weather conditions of an area and relay their findings for other climbers via Web sites and radio stations.

Rating Ice Climbs

Part of what makes ice climbing so unique is that waterfalls refreeze every year. Thus, a waterfall that froze completely solid one year can consist of thin and jagged ice the next. Because of this, there is no official standard for rating frozen waterfalls; however, many local outfitters classify the ice in their area according to their own system. Looking to explain common rating systems, Joe Josephson, one of North America's leading ice climbers, in his 1995 book *Waterfall Ice*, describes a two-part system for rating ice climbing routes. Josephson's system assesses both the overall grade of a climb—including such considerations as steepness, accessibility, length, and approximate time required to complete the climb—and the technical difficulty of the actual ice route. The first number listed in a rating is represented with a Roman numeral and refers to the grade; the second number is Arabic and refers to the route's technical difficulty.

There are six different grades to ice climbing: Grade I is the easiest and Grade VI the hardest. A Grade I route would be a climb right next to a highway or road, with an easy descent back to the bottom. A Grade VI, on the other hand, might be a waterfall high up on the side of a mountain, with a long uphill trek or ski to the base of the climb. Climbs with such grade levels may even require climbers to spend a night camping in the backcountry.

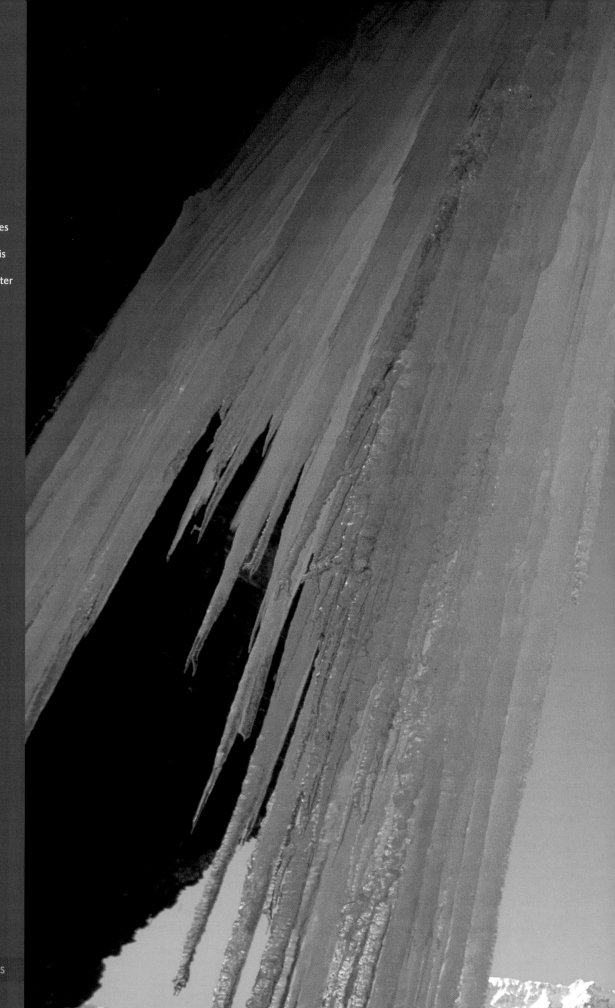

Curtains and pillars of ice are formed by collections of icicles. The core of icicles often contains water that is not frozen. This liquid center can cause icicles to snap if an ice tool is improperly inserted.

Climbers visiting Mount Cook National Park in New Zealand discover that there is more involved in their climb than ascending an ice face. A strenuous backcountry hike—often while wearing crampons—is necessary to reach the park's five glacial areas.

Climbers who do not have experience in backcountry skiing should not attempt a Grade V or VI climb.

The technical difficulty of an ice route is divided into seven levels. Level 1 climbs, which include steep, icy hills or mountains, involve basically walking on ice with crampons. Level 2 consists of 60- to 70-degree ice faces with good belay points. As the levels go up, the degree of the slope of the ice increases. A Level 7 climb is the most difficult and dangerous, involving vertical ice that may not be thick enough to hold ice screws. Very few climbers attempt such routes.

When the grade and technical difficulty level of a climb are combined, climbers have a fairly comprehensive guide to help them determine whether or not they are qualified for a specific climb. For instance, a I7 route is easy to get to, but extremely dangerous to climb. Only experts would consider attempting such a route. A VI1 route is also challenging because it requires a long approach; however, once climbers reach the base, the climb itself will involve little more than walking up a steep slope wearing crampons. Climbers with backcountry skiing skills but minimal ice climbing experience might consider attempting such a route.

Additional ratings for ice climbing include water-ice (WI) and avalanche-ice (AI) ratings. Ice climbers ascend WI, which is ice formed from rain, rivers, or run-off. Alpinists search for AI, which are sheets of ice formed by compressed snow that has re-crystallized.

Getting Started

Getting started in ice climbing is not as simple as purchasing equipment, heading out to the nearest frozen waterfall, and stabbing crampon points into the ice. Ice climbing can be extremely dangerous without the proper training and skill. Some of the world's best climbers have been killed by avalanches or falls from heights. Today, organizations and guide services throughout North America offer ice climbing classes to introduce people to the sport.

Although it helps to be located in an area where frozen waterfalls exist, there are alternatives available to the imaginative. For example, in the 1970s, a few climbers and a small adventure company called Prairie Mountaineers hosed down a cement farm silo in Minnesota in the middle of winter, building an artificial frozen waterfall on which beginning climbers could learn the art of ice climbing.

For climbers fortunate enough to live close to genuine frozen waterfalls, there is most likely a climbing guide service not far away. Some of North America's better-known ice climbing guide services include Yamnuska Inc. in the Canadian Rockies; San Juan Mountain Guides in the San Juan Mountains near Ouray, Colorado; and Chauvin Guides International, in New Hampshire's White Mountains.

Ice climbing guide services provide comprehensive training that gives individuals the instruction necessary to climb steep ice, as well as the opportunity to practice techniques in a safe and supervised manner. Climbing courses taught by expert guides provide in-depth information about fitness, clothing, equipment, and safety techniques. Depending on the length of the course, individuals may be provided with extra time to practice their skills and improve their techniques. Many guide services offer a range of courses, from one-day seminars to month-long classes. In addition, guide services often offer individual instruction courses in which a person can receive one-on-one training. Although expensive, these courses can be more efficient than a group course because the instruction is focused and intensive.

Once enrolled in a course, a new climber begins the adventure of a lifetime. The world of ice that surrounds climbing is foreign to most people.

Areas with a climate to support glaciers often have guided tours that lead travelers on ice climbs. Tourists can easily scale New Zealand's Fox Glacier (below) by means of crampons and steps that have been cut into the ice.

Climbers who are new to the sport often feel an urge to climb fast. But a slow and steady approach is best for novices, as it encourages patience and safe technique and better allows for energy conservation.

Although pictures of ice climbing terrain may suggest that it is a cold and miserable place, once climbers learn how to stay dry and warm, they begin to focus on skills and safety techniques and ignore the cold. Instruction usually begins with short lectures on the basic information and equipment needed to climb, but once this phase of the course is completed and climbers actually clip onto the rope, the adrenaline starts to flow, and the excitement becomes obvious.

As beginners start to climb, chipping their ice tools and crampons into untouched ice, they become focused on getting to the top; the higher they get off the ground, the more they want to reach the summit. Soon, their nerves kick in, and they cannot wait to reach solid ground again, so they begin to climb faster. But ascending the ice too fast is tiresome and inefficient. Climbing instructors will remind beginners to slow down and take a deep breath. They may even instruct climbers to fall on purpose at the halfway point of the climb. This helps climbers gain confidence in their equipment and belayer. With this confidence, climbers usually feel comfortable enough

When an ice climber has completed various climbing goals, the next step is to attempt more challenging climbs. Ice walls and caves in glaciers, as well as mixed climbs of ice and rock, present new obstacles for climbers to overcome.

to slow down and focus on their techniques. The more they climb, the more at ease they feel high on the side of a waterfall.

Once climbers have become proficient at the sport, they can strike out on their own. Banff National Park in Alberta, Canada, is home to the largest concentration of frozen waterfalls on the planet. Climbs of all lengths and grades, sporting names such as Weeping Wall, Polar Circus, Sea of Vapors, and Hydrophobia, can be found in this section of the Rocky Mountains. Many of the climbs are within easy walking distance of the highway. Ouray Ice Park also offers a wealth of frozen ice, with more than 130 ice climbing routes of varying difficulty levels. Since the park is funded by donations and sponsorships, there is no charge to climb. Northeastern North America offers a number of climbing locations in both the Adirondacks and the Catskills. Climbs range from easily accessible to remote and can accommodate everyone from the beginner to the expert.

The Matanuska Glacier in Alaska is an active glacier that moves one foot (30 cm) every day. The Matanuska is 24 miles (38.6 km) long and 4 miles (6.4 km) wide. This glacier is known for its bright blue color, created by densely packed glacial snow.

"Because It's There"

Famous English mountaineer George Mallory was one of the first climbers to attempt the summit of Mount Everest, the world's highest mountain, in June 1924. When asked why he wanted to climb the mountain, he responded, "Because it's there." Today, most climbers give less ambiguous answers to such questions. Karen Trank, an avid ice climber from Keene Valley, New York, sums up how she feels about climbing: "Climbers themselves are hard-pressed to explain, except to each other, the feelings that emerge when a swing of an ice tool results in a perfect 'thunk.' When the clip of a rope to an ideally placed ice screw releases a rush of tension out through their extremities, or when a series of steps leads them effortlessly to the top of a glistening blue pillar. Some climbers thrive on adrenaline rushes and personal achievement. For others, it is about immersing oneself in the beauty of the surreal crystalline ice world or communing with nature in one of its most fierce forms."

Ice climbing is obviously a great physical workout. Pulling one's body up a sheer ice face requires a great deal of strength. Long routes often demand endurance as climbers must sustain a rapid heart rate over a long period of time, sometimes for an entire day.

Ice caves and walls created by waterfalls or glaciers are formed over many years by moving water or melted snow and ice. Ice walls and caves can be found by following small creeks or streams that flow at the foot of waterfalls or glaciers.

Beyond the physical benefits of ice climbing, however, is the mental stimulation of the sport. Climbers must think constantly about where to swing ice tools or place ice screws. Route planning is critical, both before and during the climb. Climbers must carefully study a route and keep track of where they are during a climb so that they can avoid a route that is below or beyond their skill level. Getting off route on an easier climb will not provide enough challenge, and getting off route on a harder climb could be perilous.

Ice climbing can also help develop courage and confidence. Overcoming a fear of heights, for example, provides a sense of accomplishment and pride. For many climbers, climbing is an empowering experience. Today, several programs and climbing courses cater exclusively to women, allowing them to learn to climb ice in a non-competitive environment. For example, Chicks with Picks offers ice climbing courses to women in Colorado and New Hampshire. This organization and others like it have taken a male-dominated sport and helped make it more accessible and fun for women. Kim Reynolds, founder of Chicks with Picks, states that the group is "run by women for women, and provides valuable opportunities for women to gain more self confidence by meeting the natural challenges of ice climbing."

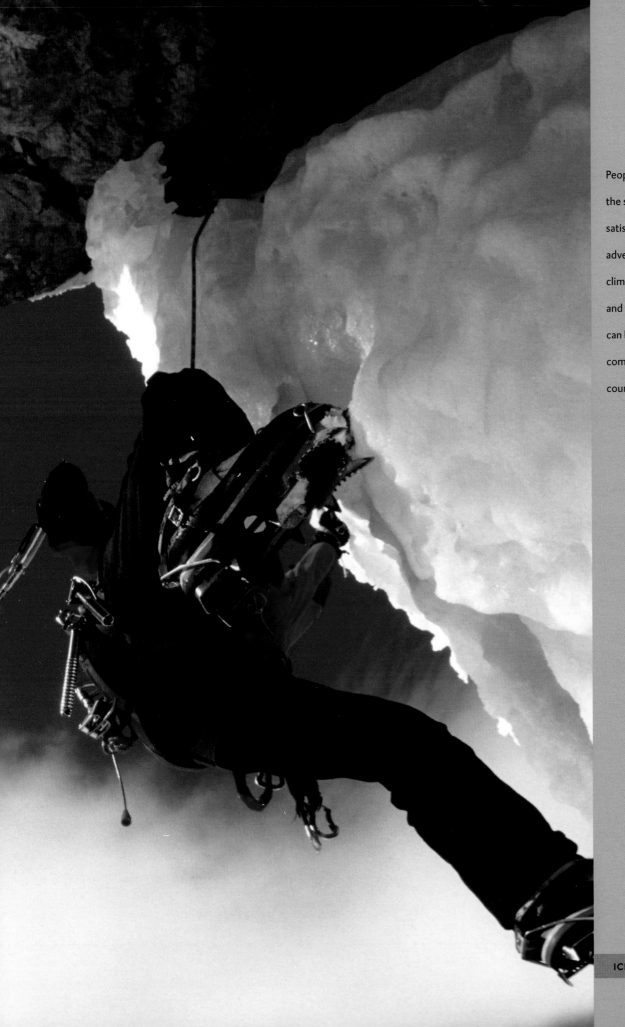

People of all ages find that the sport of ice climbing satisfies their spirit of adventure and risk. Many climb ice to release energy and face challenges that can be solved only with a combination of ingenuity, courage, and skill.

Competitions and Festivals

Most ice climbers are not satisfied to successfully summit a route and then hang up their ice tools. Part of the draw of this extreme sport is the continual challenge to become a better, stronger, and more advanced climber. As climbers continue to push themselves to climb harder and more intense routes, vertical ice climbing has developed into a serious competitive sport. In January 2005, 65 climbers from around the world arrived in Saas Fee, Switzerland, to compete in the Ice Climbing World Championships (IWC). This event, introduced in 2002, pits the world's best ice climbers against each other as they race to scale man-made, oddly shaped pillars of ice that bend and sprawl in different directions like giant spider legs.

Like most other ice climbing competitions, the IWC is broken into two categories: technical difficulty and speed. The technical difficulty competition features a vertical ice wall that tests the skills of even the most experienced climbers. Routes on these walls include several overhanging sections of ice that force climbers to move their feet above their head. Competitors in the technical difficulty category attempt to scale the ice wall as quickly as possible. If no one reaches the top, whoever climbed the highest on the route is declared the winner. The 2005 IWC men's winner in the technical difficulty event—and the only climber to reach the top of the route—was Hari Berger

Many ice climbers appreciate the solitary nature of the sport and the getaways to some of nature's quietest places. But many of those same climbers also appreciate the social fun and learning opportunities presented by ice festivals around the world.

of Austria, and the women's winner was Petra Müller of Switzerland.

The speed competition is based solely on time. All climbers attempt the same route—which is easier than the technical difficulty route—and the winner is determined by the fastest time. Speed climbing competitions vary in height depending on the available structures. The 2005 IWC speed competition was held on a 100-foot-high (30 m) ice wall built on a chicken wire frame inside a parking garage. Kryvosheytsev Evgeny of the Ukraine reached the top of this route in less than 26 seconds to win the men's competition. Russian Natalia Koulikova was the women's winner, finishing in 37 seconds.

Wherever there are frozen waterfalls, natural or man-made, there are likely to be not only climbing competitions, but also ice festivals. These events, attended by both new and experienced climbers, provide individuals with an opportunity to receive climbing instruction from expert climbers, and to observe top climbers in action as they compete for prizes. Vendors selling the most advanced equipment provide demonstrations and opportunities for participants to test the latest products. Attending an ice festival is by far the best way to learn more about ice climbing or to give this unique sport a try under the guidance of knowledgeable experts.

Hailed as the best ice festival in North America, the Ouray Ice Fest in Ouray, Colorado, is a five-day event that celebrated its 10th anniversary in January 2005. Expert climbers from around the world provide clinics and

Enduring nature's harshest elements while climbing ice on the side of a mountain may not be fun to some people. To ice climbers, though, nothing could be more stimulating. Participation in this sport grows every year as more people experience the thrill of this cold-weather sport.

slide shows for participants. The festival is packed with activities that offer something for everyone, turning this small town of 800 into a bustling crowd of 3,000 climbers, spectators, and vendors. The main attraction of this event is the climbing competition, which draws the best climbers in the world.

Another well-known ice festival takes place every February near the towns of Munising and Marquette, in the upper peninsula of Michigan. The Michigan Ice Fest is usually four days long and includes demonstrations from climbers and vendors, slide shows, and climbing clinics from expert climbers around the world. The festival features climbs up waterfalls formed along the sandstone cliffs of Lake Superior. Ranging in height from 20 to 90 feet (6–27 m), these climbs provide a variety of challenges for both novices and experts.

Today, the ice climbing community continues to grow, partly because of festivals, partly because of advancements in equipment technology (which has made tools lighter and more accessible to beginners), and partly because of increased media coverage of ice climbing events, such as IWC competitions. Ice climbing is now part of ESPN's X-Games, a televised extreme sports extravaganza that continues to grow in profile. Such media attention has exposed ice climbing to many people who had previously

From scaling the frozen waterfalls of the Canadian Rockies to maneuvering across crevasse-lined glaciers, ice climbing continues to draw adventure lovers and risk takers to challenges and obstacles that change every year.

never heard of the sport. This exposure has amplified interest in the sport, drawing larger crowds of spectators and climbers to events, competitions, and festivals worldwide.

Ice climbing's potential for growth is enormous, especially with the increased development of artificial ice walls in areas that do not feature natural frozen waterfalls. With a little ingenuity, people who live in cold-weather climates can create their own ice walls on silos or other vertical structures. Whether climbers hold a passion for natural frozen waterfalls or icy silos, they tend to be ambitious and creative types with radical ideas, and there is little doubt that they will continue to find ways to pursue and further their adventurous sport.

RECOMMENDED READING

Breashears, David, and Audrey Salkeld. *Last Climb: The Legendary Everest Expeditions of George Mallory.* Washington, D.C.: National Geographic Society, 1999.

Hattingh, Garth. *Extreme Rock and Ice: 25 of the World's Great Climbs.* Seattle: Mountaineers Books, 2000.

Josephson, Joe. *Waterfall Ice.* Calgary: Rocky Mountains Books, 1995.

Lowe, Jeff. *Ice World: Techniques and Experiences of Modern Ice Climbing.* Seattle: Mountaineers Books, 2001.

Luebben, Craig. *How to Ice Climb.* Helena, Mont.: Falcon, 1999.

WEB SITES OF INTEREST

http://www.ascendingwomen.com
Home page of Ascending Women, a women's climbing company that provides a variety of climbing classes, including rock and ice climbing.

http://www.chickswithpicks.net
Web site of Chicks with Picks, a climbing organization for women that provides ice climbing instruction.

http://gorp.away.com/gorp/activity/climb/ice_primer3.htm
Articles and information on the history of ice climbing, as well as current trends and issues in climbing.

http://www.iceclimb.com
A region-by-region description of ice climbing locations and a list of ice festivals around North America.

http://www.mountain-life.ch/iwc
Provides information about the Ice Climbing World Championships.

http://www.mountainmagic.com
A climbing equipment company offering an array of climbing gear, including state-of-the-art tools, crampons, and helmets.

http://www.rockandice.com
Home page of the climber's magazine *Rock & Ice*.

http://uiaa.ch/index.aspx
Provides a variety of information on climbing in general, as well as information on climbing competitions, including international ice climbing competitions.

GLOSSARY

adze—a cutting tool with a thin, arched blade; similar to an ax

aluminum alloy—a metal consisting of a combination of aluminum and another metal or two forms of aluminum

belay—the act of making secure; in climbing, a belay is a safety technique in which one person takes up the slack in the rope as a climber moves upward

belay device—a friction device through which the climbing rope passes; it allows the belayer to manipulate the rope and catch a climber in the event of a fall

belay point—a ledge or shelf where a climber can anchor to the ice and stand or sit in a comfortable position while belaying a second climber up

belayer—a person who pulls the slack out of a climbing rope as another climber ascends; taking up the slack rope is a safety precaution called belaying

crampons—lightweight devices with metal teeth protruding from the bottom, front, and back; they are attached to a climbing boot to gain footholds in ice

ergonomic—designed specifically for comfort and efficiency

figure eight knots—easy-to-tie knots that are shaped like a figure eight

front point—a climbing technique in which the climber faces the ice and thrusts the toes of his or her boots straight into the ice wall

hooking—a difficult climbing technique that requires climbers to lift their legs high on the ice wall, catching the rear tooth of their crampon in the ice

ice axes—long-handled ice tools with a pick on one end

ice park—a place with frozen, man-made waterfalls available for recreational climbing

ice screws—lightweight, tubular devices that are screwed into the ice and connect to a rope to protect the lead climber from falling

ice tools—short, handheld devices with sharp picks that are swung into the ice to allow climbers to pull themselves upward; they are much like ice axes, only shorter in length and lighter in weight

multi-pitch—a long climb (usually longer than the length of a climbing rope) with multiple ledges along the way, from which the lead climber can stop and belay a second climber

overhanging ice—ice that bulges out from the face of the climbing wall, forcing climbers to lean back away from the bulge in order to climb over the top of it

pitch—one length of a multi-pitch climb; often the length of a rope or the length to the first substantial ledge

plastic boots—boots that are made specifically for snow and ice climbing and feature extremely rigid soles

rappel—descend a vertical wall by sliding down a rope in a controlled manner

INDEX